THE DOORSTEP ORPHAN
EUGENE FIELD
AND A TRILOGY OF HIS BEST LOVED
POEMS

DR. JEAN A. LUKESH
Illustrated by R.E. Lukesh

Field Mouse Productions

All rights reserved. No part of this publication may be reproduced, stored in a retrieval system, or transmitted in any form or by any means, electronic, mechanical, photocopying, recording, or otherwise, without the permission in writing from the publisher/author.

Copyright © 2012 Jean A. Lukesh
Cover art and sketches copyright ©2012 by Ronald E. Lukesh
Published by Field Mouse Productions
Grand Island and Palmer, Nebraska
www.fieldmouseproductions.com
www.fieldmousebooks.com
First Printed, 2012
Printed in the United States of America
R.L.: 9.2   I.L.: 7 through adult

Lukesh, Jean A., 1950—
The Doorstep Orphan: Eugene Field and a Trilogy of His Best-Loved Poems
SUMMARY: A literary criticism biography of Eugene Field, who was known in the late 1800s and early 1900s as the Children's Poet and the Poet of Childhood, featuring three of his best-loved poems, "Little Boy Blue," "Wynken, Blynken, and Nod" (also called the "Dutch Lullaby"), and "The Duel" (also called "The Gingham Dog and the Calico Cat").
Includes selected sites, annotated reference list, endnotes, glossary, and index.
LitCritBio Series
1. Eugene Field, 1850-1895—Biography. 2. Literary Criticism. 3. Poetry, American. 4. Poets—American.—Analysis.
I. Title.   II. Subtitle.   III. Series.
E 83.866   970.06 [B] [920] [921] ISBN 978-0-9647586-5-0

Adapted from an unpublished manuscript by Jean Lukesh, Field Mouse Productions, ©1995. Field Mouse Productions, Grand Island/Palmer, Nebraska, ©2012

This
book is
dedicated
to son Lance
who also loved
"Little Boy Blue"
and took the poem
to heart just as I did,
and just as his father did
when his very own Pappy,
Emanuel or "Gabe" Lukesh,
shared it with him and listeners
on his show "Words and Music"
so many, many long years ago.
And to others of our family
who also love the poem.
JAL
REL
(2012)

Timeline of Eugene Field's Life

1850	Sept 2 or 3, Eugene Field born, St. Louis
1851	Brother Roswell (Rosy) is born
1856	Mother dies
1857-65	Gene and Rosy live with Aunt Mary and Cousin Mary or with Grandmother
1861-65	The Civil War begins and ends
1865	Gene lives with Reverend Tufts at Monson School
1867-68	Gene attends Williams College and Monson again
1869	Father dies, Eugene goes to Knox College
1870	Eugene goes to University of Missouri to be with brother
1872	Receives inheritance, becomes engaged, and travels to Europe with future brother-in-law for 6 months, spends most of his inheritance
1873	becomes a reporter at *St. Louis Evening Journal*; Oct 16, marries Julia Sutherland Comstock
1875-76	Works as editor at *St. Joseph Gazette*
1876-80	Works for two St. Louis newspapers
1879	Published his first poem "Christmas Treasures"
1880-81	Managing editor of the *Kansas City Times*
1881-83	Managing editor of *Denver Tribune*
1883	Moves to Chicago, writes "Sharps and Flats" column for morning *Chicago Daily News/Record*
1883-89	Wrote poems, short stories, and tales
1889-90	Spent 14 months in Europe for health reasons
1893-95	Writes most of his best poems and other works
1895	November 4, Eugene Field dies at his Buena Park home; buried Graceland Cemetery, Chicago
1926	Eugene Field reburied at Kenilworth Cemetery at the Church of the Holy Comforter near Chicago

Table of Contents

Chapter 1: Introducing The Children's Poet	1
Chapter 2: With Papa On The Porch	3
Chapter 3: On Cousin Mary's Doorstep	7
Chapter 4: The Curiosity Shop	11
"The Duel" or "The Gingham Dog…Calico Cat"	14
Chapter 5: On Grandmother's Doorstep	17
Chapter 6: Torn Apart By War	22
Chapter 7: Sent Away To Another School	26
Chapter 8: Off To Foreign Lands	32
Chapter 9: Building His Own Doorstep	37
Chapter 10: Columns and Foundations	41
"Little Boy Blue"	45
Chapter 11: From Poems to Books	48
Chapter 12: Family Circle	52
"Dutch Lullaby" or "Wynken, Blynken, and Nod"	56
Chapter 13: Listening to the "Dutch Lullaby"	60
Chapter 14: Home At Last, At Death's Door	63
Chapter 15: Flights of Angels	66
Chapter 16: Gift of a Child	68
Chapter 17: Others On His Doorstep	72
Chapter 18: Remembering the Poet of Childhood	75
Selected Field Sites	80
Reference List	81
End Notes	84
Glossary	88
Index	89

Eugene Field
"The Children's Poet"
1850 - 1895

sketch by Ron Lukesh

Chapter 1
Introducing The Children's Poet

"Go forth, little lyrics,...sing on, children of ours; sing to the hearts of men." So wrote Eugene Field—the man known as "The Children's Poet" and "The Poet of childhood."[1]

Field wrote those and similar words as an introduction for some of his many poems, books of poetry, essays, and articles. During the late nineteenth and early twentieth century, he and his books of nostalgic poems did indeed sing nonsense, lullabies, and tragedies to the young and the young-at-heart.

Today, few people know anything about Eugene Field, the poet or the man, or about the stories behind his words. However, many people remember bits and pieces of his works from their own childhood.

In that way, they might know the three kinds of children's poems he most often wrote—nonsense poems (such as "The Duel" also known as "The Gingham Dog and the Calico Cat"), nostalgia or tragic poems (such as "Little Boy Blue"), and lullabies (such as the "Dutch Lullaby" also known as "Wynken, Blynken, and Nod.")[2]

Readers who know Field's poetry also know a lot about the man, because as an examination of his short life clearly shows, he put many of his own memories and feelings into his poetry, especially into his three best-known, best-loved, and most memorable poems of childhood.

Chapter 2
With Papa on the Porch

In his poems, Eugene Field often tried to idealize childhood, perhaps because his own life had been rather sad and insecure. Field was born in St. Louis, Missouri, in 1850, on either the 2nd or 3rd of September—not even his friends or family agreed upon the exact date or house location.[3] Being a bit of a rascal at times, he often used that uncertainty to his advantage, allowing him to celebrate his birthday on either or both dates, as he wished.

He was the second of six children, but four of his brothers and sisters died in infancy. Eugene and younger brother Roswell (nicknamed

Rosy) were the only surviving children of the very successful lawyer Roswell Martin Field, Sr., and his second wife Frances Reed Field.[4]

When the boys were little, their papa would sit with them on the steps outside their house in St. Louis. There, father would play his violin for the neighborhood children. In those days, Papa seemed happy. He loved children and enjoyed being with them.[5] (Eugene Field would be the same way when he grew up.)

But before long, little Eugene's life would change drastically. In 1856, when he was just six and his brother Rosy was five, their mother and their new baby sister both died.[6]

His mother's loss appears to have affected Eugene greatly. During the course of his life, he would write many poems and other works dedicated to "mother," motherhood, mother figures, or mother-child love and loss. Years later, his sister-in-law wrote that he had told her, "I have carried the remembrance of [my mother's] voice and soothing touch all through my life."[7]

Gene's father probably felt the loss of his second wife just as keenly as his older son did, but he stayed very busy and tried not to show it. He would not marry again. He had already dedicated his life to his law practice by taking on the historic Dred Scott Case and other Unionist and Abolitionist causes.[8]

With his own career at stake and with America on the brink of the Civil War, Roswell Martin Field, Sr., saw that faction-ridden Missouri was no place for his two motherless boys. He loved his sons but could spend very little time with them.

At first, he left them with the servants, then later he left them with family, and then sent them to be with guardians.[9] Figuratively, if not literally, the boys became doorstep orphans—abandoned children passed along for someone else to raise.

First, Roswell, Sr., asked his sister, Mrs. Mary Jones, to take his two children into her home at Amherst, Massachusetts, and raise them there. She agreed. Aunt Mary, as she was called, was a widow who had remarried. She loved her brother's boys, but she did not have much time for them. They lived in her big house, and she was always kind and caring.[10]

Aunt Mary's adult daughter Mary Field French, who was thirty years old, also lived in the house. She generally took charge of the Field boys as a foster mother, and they loved her. They called her Cousin Mary.

Chapter 3
On Cousin Mary's Doorstep

Cousin Mary made Gene and Rosy feel safe, secure, and at home. They came to regard her as the first of their many beloved foster mothers. Some years later, Eugene even composed a poetic tribute, honoring her as "Mother."[11]

Despite her foster-mother role, Cousin Mary was an unmarried society lady when the boys lived with her. She doted on them and often took them with her when she went visiting her very proper, spinster friends.[12]

One of those friends was a woman named Lavinia Dickinson. Lavinia's sister Emily was a reclusive hermit who seldom left her room. She spent all her time writing poems, including some to a long-lost love. Only after her death did Emily Dickinson become famous as a poet.[13]

Although Eugene would grow up to be a poet and a newspaperman himself, he had limited interest in writing or in reading sad poems as a boy.[14] He and his brother had seen too much loss and sadness. Instead, they spent their time enjoying the people and activities of their new home and finding interesting things to do.

With Cousin Mary and Aunt Mary as their stabilizing forces, the Field boys enjoyed their new home and surroundings. Gene was always a natural leader, and the boys were good, but sometimes mischievous.[15] They made friends with the neighborhood children and went off together to explore nature and the numerous outbuildings in the area. They climbed trees, went fishing, or played wild Indians or pirates.[16]

Eugene even wrote plays for the neighborhood kids. (Later, he would write and perform plays in college and would sometimes do poetry and essay readings in public.)[17]

On the estate, the boys collected and kept many pets—not just Aunt Mary's canary, but also a Baltimore Oriole, a stray dog, a cat and kittens, chickens, turtles, rabbits, baby squirrels, and a little mole that Gene kept in a dresser drawer. He had names for all and wrote poems about them.[18]

Although he was afraid of the dark, Gene and his brother both loved to explore Aunt Mary's cozy rooms, dusty attics, dark cellars, and packed closets full of strange and wonderful things.[19] They especially liked her brightly-colored China plates, trunks full of family pictures, and other intriguing odds and ends.

For the rest of his life, Gene would have a fascination for collecting—such as 3,500 books—

also hundreds of clocks, figurines, envelopes, and more. The rooms in his home and office were always full of strange and remarkable items.[20]

Gene would collect toys, too, especially mechanical or moving ones. He particularly liked toy soldiers, like the tin (or pewter) figures his father sent him for Christmas. Although he loved those toy soldiers, he was always troubled by the idea of war, perhaps because he grew up during the Civil War.[21]

Over the years, Gene also collected memories. He stored all the happy times—and some of the sad and lonely ones—in his poetic memory. Sometimes in his free time, when he was able to find scraps of paper, he would write poems or draw pictures of the things he remembered.[22] Many of those memories and drawings would show up in his poetry and other writings when he became an adult, as well.

Chapter 4
The Curiosity Shop

According to one story, Cousin Mary took Gene and Rosy to see her friend Mrs. Ethan. That lady had a neighborhood store. It was a strange and wonderful place, a sort of curiosity shop.

There the boys saw all kinds of wonderfully bright, shiny things—such as art supplies, candies, candles, bottles, soaps, dolls, toys, and many other odds and ends—almost anything anyone could ever want![23] Eugene loved the place! (Years later, he would go to Europe and spend lots of time in similar shops, often bringing back strange souvenirs to add to his own collections.)

To Gene and Rosy, the most fascinating

items in Mrs. Ethan's store were on the fireplace mantle. There stood an odd-looking cuckoo clock with a carved face and white numerals. The clock was surrounded by two strange-looking cloth creatures with polka-dot bodies, shoe-button eyes, and scarlet-red tongues.[24]

Little Rosy waited until he left the shop, then he asked about the strange things on the mantle. Cousin Mary informed him that the creatures were cats or dogs made of quilt scraps. Mrs. Ethan had been making and selling such homemade stuffed toys for years.

According to one account of the visit, Rosy then wished aloud that he could have one of those "gingham cats-or-dogs." But suddenly he stopped, and wide-eyed, asked his big brother Gene if the stuffed animals were alive.

Eugene, always the imaginative jokester, reportedly answered something like, "They're alive, alright. At night when it's dark, they fight. Then they eat each other up." Perhaps Gene even scared himself; he was always afraid of the dark.[25]

Most likely it is from the memory of that day or a similar one that the poem, "The Duel," was born. That was the poem's real name, but most people know it better by its first line, "The Gingham Dog and the Calico Cat."

Although that poem was written many years later, it appears that some of Gene's experiences and memories are clearly recognizable in it, from the time when he and Rosy lived as boys with the two Marys. Objects from their house, including Aunt Mary's China plates, and things from Mrs. Ethan's store appear to be most prominent, especially the gingham dog, the calico cat, the Dutch clock, and of course, Gene's story to Rosy of how the cat and the dog ate each other up.

This is how that poem goes:

THE DOORSTEP ORPHAN 14

"The Duel" — Known as
"The Gingham Dog and the Calico Cat"

The gingham dog and the calico cat
Side by side on the table sat;
"Twas half-past twelve and (what do you think!)
Nor one nor t'other had slept a wink!
The old Dutch clock and the Chinese plate
Appeared to know as sure as fate
There was going to be a terrible spat.

THE DOORSTEP ORPHAN

(I wasn't there; I simply state
What was told to me by the Chinese plate!)

The gingham dog went "bow-wow-wow!"
And the calico cat replied "mee-ow!"
The air was littered, an hour or so,
With bits of gingham and calico,
While the old Dutch clock in the chimney-place
Up with its hands before its face,
For it always dreaded a family row!
(Now mind: I'm only telling you
What the old Dutch clock declares is true!)

The Chinese plate looked very blue,
And wailed, "Oh dear! What shall we do!"
But the gingham dog and the calico cat
Wallowed this way and tumbled that,
Employing every tooth and claw
In the awfullest way you ever saw—

And, oh! how the gingham and calico flew!

(Don't fancy I exaggerate—

I got my news from the Chinese plate!)

Next morning, where the two had sat

They found no trace of dog or cat;

And some folks think unto this day

That burglars stole that pair away!

But the truth about the cat and pup

Is this: they ate each other up!

Now what do you really think of that!

(The old Dutch clock it told me so,

And that is how I came to know.)

Chapter 5
On Grandmother's Doorstep

Eugene and Rosy lived happily with their aunt and cousin for a while. Then one day their grandmother, Esther Kellogg Field, came to visit. While there, Grandmother, a very strict and proud New England Puritan, saw Gene pretending to read—possibly with his book upside down, reciting by memory. She also found that he could not tell time.[26] She worried that his schooling was inadequate, and some accounts say she voiced her concern to Eugene's father.

The father—Roswell Martin Field, Sr.—and his own brother had both been good but mischievous boys themselves. However, their esteemed family had intended great things for them and had sent them off to school at an early age. As expected, Roswell, Sr., had done well in school, and had even gone away to college while very young to learn the practice of law and to become a lawyer and judge.[27]

So Roswell Martin Field, Sr., expected good things from his own sons and told them so in his letters, especially in those written in formal Latin to Eugene when he was a little older. When Roswell heard that his sons needed more education, he wrote back to the ladies of the family, asking Grandmother (or else giving her permission) to take his children to her home and educate them over the summer.[28]

The boys missed their two Marys, but they came to enjoy living on their Grandmother's three-acre homestead in Newfane, Vermont, for several months. Gene also missed his faithful dog, Dooley, so he wrote one of his first poems in honor of the dog.[29] Memories, faithful pets, and toy dogs would be a part of his poems for the rest of his life.

The Field boys also collected many other pets at Grandmother's estate—not only dogs, but also cats, pigeons, a goat, a donkey, chipmunks, rabbits, grasshoppers, lizards, a white mouse that Gene kept in his pocket, and other animals. Gene and Rosy thought the animals had human characteristics, so they gave them funny names and made up fantasy stories about them.[30]

Gene's late grandfather had also kept a collection of things in his old museum on the estate—fossils, rocks, butterflies, bugs, birds' eggs, and more. Gene liked studying those items, and he became interested in collecting some of them, too.[31]

Grandmother, though, insisted religiously that the boys must put their minds to better use.

She required Gene to read from the Bible, and she paid him to write Bible-related verses for her. She also had him carry her footstove and snacks to church for her, so she could keep her feet warm and her stomach from rumbling.[32]

After a while, Gene found he had a talent for writing—Bible verses, plays, poems, even a little newspaper—but Grandmother expected still greater things from him. After all, the Field family had many distinguished ancestors—a famous London astronomer of the 1600s, some of the first Puritan settlers of New England, and several doctors, lawyers, and scientists.[33]

Eugene's father had even been a brilliant young scholar himself. From a very early age, he loved literature and was well-versed in five languages—Greek, Latin, French, German, and English. He had entered college at age 11, graduated at 15, became a lawyer at 17 or 18, served as a member of the Vermont General Assembly before the age of 30, and was elected state attorney several times.[34]

After a very brief and bitter first marriage to Mary Almira Phelps, he moved to Missouri in 1839 and became a famous lawyer.[35] Later he married Frances Reed who became the mother of his only surviving children, Gene and Roswell, Jr.

Gene and Rosy were both intelligent boys, but they were not as academically motivated or professionally dedicated as their father and uncle had been. So Gene's father and grandmother insisted that the boys should spend several hours a day studying.

After several months at Grandmother's estate, the boys returned to Cousin Mary's house. Years later, they would go to boarding school, then college. But before that, the Civil War tore America apart.

Chapter 6
Torn Apart By War

Eugene Field was not quite eleven when the Civil War started—states fighting against states, brothers fighting against brothers, and neighbors and friends going off to join up and fight in the army. It was a tragic and troubling time for a boy like Eugene who hated war, a boy who had always been very close to his only brother, and who longed for his absent father, a father caught up in the politics of the war.[36]

Gene's father had tried to keep the Civil War from happening. Between 1853 and 1857, he had worked, free of charge, to help a slave named Dred Scott who had lived in free states and who wanted to remain free. Finally, his case went to the U.S. Supreme Court. There it was lost, when the Chief Justice, a Southerner, ruled that slaves were not citizens and had no rights. As a result, Dred Scott became a slave—and was considered property—again.

Afterwards Roswell Martin Field, Sr., returned to his law practice in Missouri, a very dangerous place to be in those days. He continued his work to help free the slaves and to hold the Union together. That brought him fame, but also took a great toll on him, turning him into a recluse, separated from society and his family. The stress literally ate away at his health.[37]

Then, just as the Civil War was ending, a terrible thing happened. Gene and his friends heard about it when they found Deacon Spencer crying uncontrollably in his horse-drawn buggy. He told them that President Lincoln had been assassinated.

Eugene had admired Lincoln. That incident stuck in his mind and became a story he would tell into adulthood. It is no wonder that Eugene Field often said that he hated war and guns.[38]

After the Civil War, when Gene was about fifteen, he and Rosy were once again sent away from home by their father. This time they went to live with the Reverend James Tufts, at his small private school in Monson, Massachusetts. Tufts would become their new guardian and teacher. He was a friend of their father's and had been told to separate the two brothers.[39]

Gene lived with the Tufts family. They were always nice to him, but he was very homesick. He hated studying and being in a classroom, so he used his time unwisely, either drawing or playing pranks. He loved being with his brother and being outside, but school left him little time for that.

One day, he had had enough. He decided to

run away from school, but Rosy refused to go with him, so he went alone, before dawn. Gene walked all day long along the railroad tracks. Finally, he reached Aunt Mary's house, twenty-five miles away. (Each mile had contained 2500 railroad ties to the mile, he knew that because he had counted them.)[40]

When he arrived there, Aunt Mary felt so sorry for him and for his sore feet and his empty stomach, that she said he did not have to go back to school. However, the more practical Cousin Mary said Gene had been sent to school to study, and to learn to be more responsible. She said he had not learned those lessons or many others, so he must return to school—on the next train—after he had eaten and rested.[41]

He did that, but he never learned to like school and always felt that his real education actually started after he left college.

Chapter 7
Sent Away to Another School

When Gene was 17, his grandmother died. The next year, he was sent to Williams College, where he spent only eight months. There, the intelligent but mischievous young man continued to use his new-found writing talents and his clever imagination to rebel and enjoy himself.[42]

In college, Gene loved to put on humorous skits and dramas, to play good-natured tricks, and to write satirical humor. Surprisingly, he found he loved to read, but his mind was seldom on his studies even though instructors and their families often took him in and tried to help him adjust to school.

He would attend at least four private schools or colleges as a young adult—Monson (twice), Williams, Knox, and the University of Missouri. He would have guardians at each—but he graduated from none of them.[43]

He was just not interested in grades. However, he was interested in entertaining people and giving humorous opinions and observations on any topic, especially politics and government, in the classroom or on the public stage and later in the newspapers.

Some of his professors even noted that they would not be surprised to find Eugene Field writing professionally someday.[44] Before long, Gene proved them right by taking a job as a columnist, a job that paid him to write his own brand of biting humor on a variety of topics.

Later in his adult life, Gene would even make his living writing poems and articles for newspapers all across the Midwest—from St. Louis to St. Joseph to Kansas City, and from Denver to Chicago. He would be very good at his craft, and he thoroughly enjoyed writing humorous stories and good-natured but satirical poetry that made fun of the rich and famous, especially entertainers, politicians, and even other authors.

But in the meantime, Eugene did not do so well at Williams College. He did not care to study and spent so much time having fun that the administrators at Williams recommended that Gene should return to Monson and Reverend Tufts' guardianship.[45]

Though outwardly a happy person, Eugene had many secret heartaches. He keenly missed his father and felt that he, his brother, and their father had all suffered greatly as a result of Mother's death, the war, and separation from each other.[46]

Things would get worse. On July 21, 1869,

when Gene was nearly 19, his father died of physical exhaustion, possibly complicated by throat cancer.[47] Hundreds of people attended the funeral, praising Roswell Martin Field, Sr., as an intellectual, a scholar, and a great humanitarian. At that time, Gene realized what a great man his father had been. At the same time, he mourned for the father he had loved but only known from a distance.[48]

Not long after the funeral, Gene started at a new school, Knox College in Galesburg, Illinois. There, he continued to waste time, while Rosy, the "other doorstep orphan," was doing well at the University of Missouri.[49] Gene enjoyed some of his classes but was not serious about his studies, despite living with professors and their families.

Those adults often mentored Gene and became close friends of his, but they could not motivate him to finish his schooling. He was just having too much fun. Then, around the age of twenty, he transferred to the University of Missouri to be closer to his brother Rosy.

Gene was nearing his twenty-first birthday and would soon be inheriting money from his father's will. That money and some property had been held in trust for him (and for Rosy and the Marys) by his father's friend Melvin Gray. Gray had also been Gene's guardian at Knox College.[50] (Gene would be an adult before he realized just how much Melvin Gray had helped him throughout his life.)

Anticipating his inheritance, Gene and his own good friend and fellow-student Edgar Comstock decided that they would soon quit school and tour Europe together—at Gene's expense. In the meantime, they went home to visit Comstock's family in St. Joseph. There, Gene met all of Edgar's family, including his parents, two brothers, and five sisters.

Gene loved the Comstock family and felt right at home with them. He enjoyed their many activities and was comfortable there. Soon he fell in love with Julia, one of the youngest sisters.[51]

Gene and Edgar still had plans to travel across Europe, but those plans might well have changed quickly at that point if Julia had not been too young to get married. Her father liked Gene well enough, but he knew the young man had no diploma, no home of his own, no money, and no steady job.

Gene tried to remedy part of that deficiency. He tried out for a professional acting career but failed, so he returned to college to wait for his inheritance and his future bride.[52]

Chapter 8
Off To Foreign Lands

Separated by death from his own father and nearing the age of 21 when he would receive that inheritance, Eugene may have felt both lost and surprisingly empowered. He no longer needed to follow in his father's footsteps and was free to choose his own way to go.[53]

Near that time, he and his friend Edgar left college for good. They went back to Edgar's family home in St. Joseph to wait for the money. Gene, Julia, and her family all enjoyed their time together.

When the money came to him, Gene decided that if Julia was still too young to marry, then he and Edgar should go on to Europe and give Julia time to grow up. So Gene took Edgar and Ida, one of Edgar's oldest sisters, to visit Aunt Mary and Cousin Mary. Then they continued on to New York to visit Comstock relatives.

From there, Gene and Edgar intended to take a steamship to Europe, but before their ship came in, Gene went off on one of his side trips. At that point, he posted a letter back to Edgar and Ida at the place where they were staying, saying that something important had forced him to return to Missouri temporarily on business.[54]

Gene's idea of serious business was a marriage proposal to Julia. Toward that purpose, he quickly returned to St. Joseph, 1500 miles away, to become engaged. Then he hurriedly traveled back to New York in time to meet Edgar and board the ship to Europe.

Eugene and Edgar had a wonderful time in

Europe, six months in Ireland, England, France, and Italy. They saw many grand sights, rescued a dog that was being beaten (Gene loved dogs and could never stand to see them abused), visited old-country shops, collected books and strange souvenirs—and spent thousands of dollars, or nearly all of his inheritance.[55]

Gene had never been good with money and never would be. He came home broke but happy, with an odd assortment of items to add to his collections. He even brought home a French poodle for Julia.[56]

After returning to America, Eugene went looking for a way to make a living. He had written for college newspapers, so before long he found a job, working for a St. Louis paper. That would become the perfect career for him. He would be a newspaperman for the rest of his life.

He and Julia were still in love, but her

parents insisted that she wait to marry until she turned eighteen. After Gene received a promotion at the newspaper, he and Julia were finally allowed to wed. Julia was then almost seventeen.[57]

After receiving some more money from Melvin Gray, Gene took his bride to New York on their honeymoon. A romantic, and a boy at heart, Gene then spent all that money with no thought of how he and Julia would live when they came home. His good friend Slason Thompson later said, "Eugene Field would have been a boy at fifty and at eighty had he lived [that long.]"[58]

More responsible and far wiser than her years, Julia soon recognized her husband's lack of financial sense. She then took over the bill-paying, as well as the housekeeping, and later the child-rearing.[59] If Eugene Field were to be the ever-mischievous, never-grow-up Peter Pan hero and leader of her new family, then she would be the more realistic and stabilizing Wendy-like homebody of his.

Even so, neither of them ever had a realistic head for finances, and Field never made much money, especially as their family grew so large so soon. As a result, they often lived from paycheck to paycheck.

Chapter 9
Building His Own Doorstep

A love of children and childhood became evident in much of what Eugene Field did from then on. On the day he married his beloved young bride, Julia Sutherland Comstock (Edgar's sister), the new groom was late to his own wedding.

He had stopped on the way to break up a fight between two little boys. He then paid the boys to go have ice cream and be good. After brushing off his own clothes, Gene went on to the ceremony, then sat through a majority of the wedding supper holding the minister's small son adoringly.[60]

The following year, the newlyweds were

blessed with their own firstborn son, Roswell Martin Field (named for Gene's father and brother), but the baby only lived two months. According to Gene's sister-in-law, that death greatly affected Eugene Field.[61] Shortly thereafter, he wrote what he called his first truly serious poem, called "Christmas Treasures."

Though not considered a classic, the poem was important as the fore-runner of several of his later poems, such as "Little Boy Blue," "Wynken, Blynken, and Nod," and others.[62] Personally, "Christmas Treasures" was important to Field, as his own heartfelt tribute to his little lost son.

The death of that firstborn son saddened Eugene Field, but it also strengthened his devotion to his growing family. Then, one year after his son's death, his first daughter was born. Gene and his wife christened the baby Mary French Field, after his beloved Cousin Mary. Gene nicknamed his daughter "Trotty" and usually called her by that name.

Gene doted on Trotty but was also overjoyed a year later when another son, Melvin Gray Field, was born. Named after Melvin Gray, the family friend and one of Eugene's most respected guardians, baby Melvin was the only Field child so serious and so respected that he was never given a funny nickname.[63]

An unusual thing happened the year Melvin was born. "April Vespers," one of Eugene's poems, was published in Europe where it became very popular. However, the poem was credited to an English composer, Sir William S. Gilbert. Gilbert and his partner, Sir Arthur Sullivan—or Gilbert and Sullivan—were world famous at that time for their very popular, light operas.[64]

Rather than being angry that his poem was credited to someone else, Field felt flattered, amused, and honored by the miscredit.⁶⁵ To acknowledge it, Field gave his next son Eugene, Jr., the nickname of "Pinny"—that was short for one of Gilbert and Sullivan's most popular operettas, *H.M.S. Pinafore*.

Gene's reputation as a writer, and his family, were both growing quickly. Soon, another son, Frederick Skiff Field, was born. The baby was nicknamed "Daisy," because he had huge daisy-like blue eyes and because of a popular song of the time called "Oh My! Ain't He a Daisy."⁶⁶

Field loved to be with all his children, and he made time for all of them. His children were almost like his pets from his childhood days, and he called each of them except Melvin by their cute little baby names. He bounced them on his knee, held them in his lap, sang to them, and constantly created stories and poems for them. He even wrote about them in the newspapers.

Chapter 10
Columns and Foundations

Surrounded by his beloved family, Eugene Field counted his many blessings, but his heartaches continued, as well. His newspaper column was widely quoted, and he had become one of the first nationally known columnists. So, against the advice of his editor, he decided to write and publish a book, a satire on Chicago society.[67]

From the first, there were many problems. The book did not sell well, even though it contained a foreword written by his friend Julian Hawthorne, who was the gifted son of the very popular author Nathaniel Hawthorne. Field then began to question his own writing ability.[68]

Other personal complications also arose. A second baby daughter died soon after birth, and Gene experienced severe physical and emotional problems of his own.

Depressed, anxious, and grief-stricken, he began to suffer more and more from stomach troubles, heart problems, and lack of sleep. Gene was slim and never a very healthy man. He was six feet tall and weighed only 160 pounds.

His job with the newspaper required him to be out in public and society for long hours. There, he ate and drank too much. As such, he was often ill with even more digestive problems that would plague him for the rest of his life.[69]

During one sleepless night when he needed to finish a poem for a publishing deadline, he drew upon the grief that had helped him create his first melancholy poem, "Christmas Treasures." He then wrote the poignant and profoundly moving poem,

"Little Boy Blue."[70]

The poem told the story of a father longing for his little son who had died. Field put a lot of himself into the poem—his own feelings and remembrances of his lost children, his own lost childhood, and even, perhaps, his lost parents.

He put some of his own childhood toys into it, too—a faithful toy dog and the toy soldiers his absentee-father had sent him for Christmas. Drawing on those memories, he illustrated the poem with his own sketches of the dog and soldier.

When he finished "Little Boy Blue," Field gave the hand-written, author-illustrated copy of the poem to his friend and co-worker Slason Thompson. Thompson crossed out a few words in the next to last line and made changes in his own handwriting.[71] The edited poem was then published in several newspapers.

More than any other poem, "Little Boy

Blue" helped establish Eugene Field as a respected poet and a significant American writer of the late nineteenth and early twentieth century. Its popularity soon eclipsed that of the poems of James Russell Lowell, the major poet of the time.[72]

Soon after that, critics noted that Field's dusty little toy dog and rusted toy soldier had become the universal symbols of grief for anyone mourning a lost child.

Field's friend Slason Thompson said the poem "played with exquisite tenderness on the heartstrings." He believed the title summed up the tragedy, pain, and wonder "of Death taking the innocent and leaving the parents [to wonder about] the mystery of 'What has become of our Little Boy Blue [s]ince he kissed them [the little toy soldier and the little toy dog] and put them there?'"[73]

That poem follows:

THE DOORSTEP ORPHAN 45

"Little Boy Blue"

The little toy dog is covered with dust,
But sturdy and staunch he stands;
And the little toy soldier is red with rust,
And his musket molds in his hands.

THE DOORSTEP ORPHAN 46

Time was when the little toy dog was new,
And the soldier was passing fair;
And that was the time when our Little Boy Blue
Kissed them and put them there.

"Now don't you go till I come," he said,
"And don't you make any noise!"
So, toddling off to his trundle-bed,
He dreamt of the pretty toys;
And, as he was dreaming, an angel song
Awakened our Little Boy Blue—
Oh! the years are many, the years are long,
But the little toy friends are true!

Aye, faithful to Little Boy Blue they stand,
Each in the same old place—
Awaiting the touch of a little hand,
The smile of a little face;
And they wonder,

as waiting the long years through
In the dust of that little chair,
What has become of our Little Boy Blue,
Since he kissed them and put them there.

Chapter 11
From Poems To Books

Although Field's friend Slason Thompson later said that "Little Boy Blue" was not the author's best work, still Thompson quickly recognized the poem as a popular masterpiece of great and lasting value.

In 1889, Thompson began collecting small amounts of money from friends to have that poem and several other Field poems, including the "Dutch Lullaby" but not "The Duel," published in two books called *The Little Book of Western Verse* (dedicated to Cousin Mary French) and *The Little Book of Profitable Tales*. Of all Field's books, *The Little Book of Western Verse* is generally considered the best and most popular collection of his work.[74]

Despite the popularity of "Little Boy Blue" and *The Little Book of Western Verse*, Eugene Field never had very much money, and he was often ill. When his doctor suggested he take an extensive European vacation for rest, Field said he could not stand to be away from his children. Although he knew it would be very expensive, he decided to take his whole family along with him.[75]

As a result, the children attended school in Germany, while Eugene and his wife Julia toured Belgium, England, France, Germany, Holland, and Scotland for 14 months. There they met with famous writers, such as Oscar Wilde and Sir Arthur Conan Doyle. Gene wrote poems and articles and sent them back to the newspaper for publication.[76]

Eugene's health, though, did not improve on

that vacation. Still physically ill, he became more and more homesick for his sons and daughter in Germany. Finally, he and his wife decided to rejoin the children, . . .about the time they received word their oldest son Melvin, age 13, had suddenly become very ill and was not expected to live.[77]

The boy died soon after that, and the grieving family took his body home to Chicago for the funeral. Eugene Field then mourned for another of his sons, another "Little Boy Blue."

According to Slason Thompson—Field's friend and often his biographer—Melvin's death was the worst of all Eugene Field's many tragedies.[78] Once again, Field had lost another of his beloved children.

Eugene then dedicated his next book, *With Trumpet and Drum*, a book of children's poems (that also did not contain "The Duel") published in 1892, to his son Melvin. In a dedication nearly as tragic and thought-provoking as his "Little Boy Blue," Field wrote the following bitter-sweet lines:

> Ah me! But a love that is sweeter than mine
> Holdeth my boy in his keeping today,
> And my heart it is lonely.

His pain and eloquence were obvious.

Chapter 12
Family Circle

In an effort to try to get over his depression, Field drew his family ever closer around him for the next few years. He doted on his remaining children, including the two newest, another son Roswell Francis Field, nicknamed "Po" or "Posy" to rhyme with Rosy, born in 1893, and Ruth Gray, or "Sister Girl," born in 1895.

Field and his family had moved often, as he worked on one newspaper after another—from St. Louis to St. Joseph, back to St. Louis, then on to Kansas City, Denver, and finally Chicago.[79]

Unlike his own father who had withdrawn from his children into his work, Eugene often took his work home with him, to be closer to his family. His world revolved around his writing and his children, and he included them in any way he could. He immersed himself in the world of his children and often wrote poems and other works about them and for them. Soon people began to call him "The Children's Poet" or "The Poet of Childhood."[80]

At home, he always seemed to be surrounded by children—his own, and the neighbor kids, too. All children seemed to be welcome there. He invented games for them to play, and he played games with them. Although never athletic, he loved baseball and enjoyed officiating at the neighborhood baseball games.[81]

He also read to the children, told them stories, and gave them almost anything they wanted. He even kept closets full of toys for them to play with, and he gave away new dolls and bags of marbles to any children who came to visit. Making children happy made Gene feel like a happy child, too.[82]

Gene seemed to collect children, but he also collected all kinds of other things, as if he were trying, in some way, to regain his own childhood. He had shelves full of toys, especially mechanical toys, books, pewter figurines, clocks, bottles, and other curios. Such things always filled his houses and made them resemble Mrs. Ethan's old store.

His brother Rosy later said that Eugene "took boyish pleasure" in the "toys and trinkets of children which seemed to" inspire his poetry and make it more effective. Rosy noted that those "weird dolls and absurd toys" were the ties that bound Gene to the children, and "each trumpet and drum,…each little toy dog, each little tin soldier"—each a remembrance of Gene's own childhood—"played its part in the poems he sent out into the world."[83]

Souvenirs collected from foreign countries also played a part in his writings. Many of those showed up in his lullaby poems of England, Scotland, Japan, Norway, Cornwall, Sicily, Orkney, and Armenia. In a late nineteenth- and early twentieth-century home so full of children, lullaby songs and poems were well known and common. Indeed, Eugene Field wrote many of those, and filled them with things he had collected.

One such souvenir was a wooden shoe that may well have served as the inspiration for his poem, a "Dutch Lullaby." That very popular work also became known by its first line, "Wynken, Blynken, and Nod." Field said it was his favorite poem.[84]

Although a lullaby on many levels, that work is also a skillfully crafted piece of symbolism and wordplay—as can be seen here:

THE DOORSTEP ORPHAN 56

"The Dutch Lullaby" — Known as
"Wynken, Blynken, and Nod"

Wynken, Blynken, and Nod one night

Sailed off in a wooden Shoe—

Sailed on a river of crystal light,

Into a sea of dew.

"Where are you going, and what do you wish?"

The old moon asked the three.

"We have come to fish for the herring-fish
That live in this beautiful sea;
Nets of silver and gold have we,"
Said Wynken,
Blynken,
And Nod.

The old moon laughed and sang a song,
As they rocked in the wooden shoe;
And the wind that sped them all night long
Ruffled the waves of dew;
The little stars were the herring-fish
That lived in that beautiful sea.
"Now cast your nets whenever you wish—
But never afeard are we";
So cried the stars to the fishermen three,
Wynken,
Blynken,
And Nod.

All night long their nets they threw
To the stars in the twinkling foam,
Then down from the sky
came the wooden shoe,
Bringing the fisherman home;
"Twas all so pretty a sail, it seemed
As if it could not be;
And some folk thought 'twas a dream they'd
dreamed
Of sailing that beautiful sea;
But I shall name you the fishermen three:
Wynken,
Blynken,
And Nod.

Wynken and Blynken are two little eyes,
And Nod is a little head,
And the wooden shoe that sailed the skies

THE DOORSTEP ORPHAN

Is the wee one's trundle-bed.
So shut your eyes while mother sings
Of wonderful sights that be,
And you shall see the beautiful things
As you rock in the misty sea,
Where the old shoe rocked the fishermen three,
Wynken,
Blynken,
And Nod.

Chapter 13
Listening To the "Dutch Lullaby"

In the "Dutch Lullaby" poem, Eugene Field's tenderness for and dedication to children is evident. He loved to wrap his own children in his arms and hold them close, to make up lullaby songs or poems for them, and to rock them in their wooden-shoe-like cradles and trundle-beds. In essence, he longed to give them that gentle and soothing closeness and security he had known so fleetingly as a child.

In the poem, the old moon could be a mother's face as the child looks up to see her. And the moon's laughing and singing could be a mother's own sweet lullaby, the sleep song of a loving parent—something often missing from Field's own childhood.

The herring-fish following in the wake of the adventurer's shoe-like ship across the deep night-blue (of sea or sky) may be the reflected stars, or even wishes waiting to come true. The gold and silvery nets cast across the sky are the galaxies of stars and planets seen in the "crystal light" of the Milky Way or in the gold of a late sunset or morning sky. The little bed is a floating boat, gently rocking to keep the children safe all night and to bring them safely home at dawn.

Field often wrote while in his own bed, perhaps while imagining he heard his own mother's lullaby song. He said he wrote the "Dutch Lullaby" after waking from sleep, and sitting straight up in bed to write it down. He originally wrote, "into a sea of blue," but changed and transitioned it to "a sea of dew" the following morning.⁸⁵

In the poem, Field also used wordplay to describe the three little friends—Wynken, Blynken, and Nod—names that led to the obvious winkin', blinkin', and nod of "two little eyes" and "a little head" of a sleepy child, cuddled and safe. Gene had held many of his own children and watched them nod off to sleep in his loving arms. Others he could only hold in his memories.

In all, the lullaby shows itself as a glorious unending representational or symbolic love poem between parent and child.

Chapter 14
Home At Last, At Death's Door

Eugene Field always longed to give his children the permanence he had never known as a child or as an adult. As an orphaned child, he had lived with one relative or guardian after another. As an adult—a newspaperman—he had moved his wife and children from one rented home to another from the East to the West and back again. However, his dream had always been to give them a real home of their own, a place like Aunt Mary's house or Grandmother's homestead.

In 1895, though he called himself a Westerner, Gene found just the place he wanted. He moved his family into a big, old country house he called Sabine Farm at Buena Park, near Chicago, Illinois.[86] A vast menagerie of pets, resembling the ones from Aunty's acreage and Grandmother's yard, including a goat and a donkey, came to live at the farm and frolic there.

Eugene had not been well for six years, and he still missed his three children who had died young. But he, Julia, and their five surviving children—Mary (Trotty), Eugene, Jr. (Pinny), Frederick (Daisy), Roswell (Posy), and Ruth (Sister Girl)—all loved living on the farm—even though it required a lot of repair work. Even brother Rosy lived nearby, to be close, and to work with Gene on poetry and book projects. The brothers had always been close whenever they could be.[87]

The family had not been living at their farm for more than a few months when Eugene fell ill again. He had recently gotten over a bout with pneumonia and had a separate bedroom in the house, so that he could read or write in bed on nights when he could not sleep. Because Eugene often felt unwell, was afraid of the dark, and hated being alone, his son Daisy slept in the room, too.[88]

On November 3rd, 1895, Gene felt unwell again and stayed in bed all day. The doctor made a house call on that date, telling him it was nothing much. Other visitors came in, noting that it was a beautiful day. Eugene agreed, but remarked mysteriously that "This is the season when things die....We may hear of many deaths tomorrow."[89]

After the visitors left, the ailing Field finished his day's correspondence and his newspaper column. Then at bedtime, he called out to his family, "Good night, my dears!" and went to sleep, with his young son Daisy nearby in the same room.

Chapter 15

Flights of Angels

Just before dawn the following morning, 45-year-old Eugene Field turned over in his sleep, gave a soft sigh, and breathed no more. Daisy heard him and lovingly reached over to touch his father's hand—but he received no response. Frightened, Daisy called out to the rest of the family that he believed his papa was dead.

Papa had indeed died, with a smile upon his lips. Heart failure, the doctor noted.[90] As it had been with Gene's own father's passing, Eugene Field's body had just worn out from physical exhaustion. As his friend Slason Thompson said, "It was just such a death as [the ailing Field] often said would be his choice. Just a dropping off to sleep here and an awakening yonder."[91]

Eugene Field had gone to be with his "Little Boy Blue" and with his two other lost children and with the other angels that had so often decorated his poetry. Perhaps a pleasant dream had just called him away, and a child or angel had come to lead him through green pastures and by still waters.

The following Monday, the *Chicago Tribune* did not carry Field's usual "Sharps and Flats" column. In its place, the newspaper printed two of his most-famous and best-loved poems, "Little Boy Blue" and "Wynken, Blynken, and Nod"—also known as the "Dutch Lullaby"—Field's favorite work.[92]

Chapter 16
Gift of a Child

A few days later, Eugene Field, "the Poet of Childhood," was laid to rest holding a single white rose, the gift of a special but anonymous child.

According to the legend, on the day before the funeral, a friend of the Field family went to the florist to order flowers for the ceremony. While there, the woman noticed that a little girl, dressed in rags, had timidly followed her into the shop.

"Are those flowers for Mr. Field?" the little girl asked with sorrowful eyes. "Oh, I wish I could send him one! Please could I have just one?" With that, the florist gave the child a big, beautiful, single white rose, that the waif handed to the friend, asking her to "please put this flower near Mr. Field."

The friend decided the white rose—a symbol of purity, innocence, and love—should be placed very near Eugene Field. In fact, it was placed in the very hand that had often held a pen to write so many poems of love for the children of the world, as a special tribute from a special admirer.[93]

Eugene Field, the "Children's Poet," was then buried in Graceland Cemetery, in Chicago, near his beloved son Melvin who had died just a few years before. That pleasant peaceful cemetery abounded with birds and nature and seemed quite appropriate as a resting place for the beloved poet who loved nature so much.

As Field had noted in a letter to his friend Slason Thompson, "The [cemetery] lot I selected and bought is in a pretty, accessible spot, sheltered by two oak trees, just such a spot as the boy himself, with his love for nature, would have chosen."⁹⁴ That was also just such a spot as Gene would have selected for the boy in himself, and it became his resting place beside his son.

Slason Thompson wrote that "It is a quiet spot..., in a lovely little glade, away from the sorrowful processions of the main driveways." There, "leafy branches wave above his grave shielding it from the glare of the sun in summer and the rude sweep of the winds in winter."⁹⁵

But Eugene was not to be in that leafy glade or by his son's side at Graceland for long. In 1913 Field's friend Thompson and two other men went to visit Gene's grave at Graceland. They found the neighborhood changed and the grave poorly marked. Before long, there arose a campaign to put up a more appropriate monument at the gravesite and another one at Lincoln Park where Field had often taken his own children.⁹⁶

Eugene's son-in-law was in charge of a more affluent church. Soon a committee decided Field deserved to be reburied in a "more dignified" church cemetery, among more noted individuals. So on March 7, 1926, Eugene Field's body was moved to Kenilworth Cemetery, near Chicago.[97]

The reburial ceremony was well attended, and Eugene Field was laid to rest to the sound of his famous poem "Little Boy Blue." Afterward, the Poet of Childhood, was a doorstep orphan again. He was gone, but not yet forgotten—left alone again, far from home, in a strange place with no family or friends nearby, "in a suburb of Chicago, that never knew him and which he never knew."[98]

Then in 1936, Gene's beloved wife Julia died. She was buried at Kenilworth Cemetery next to her husband.[99] In death, she had finally been brought to his doorstep where they could be together forever.

Chapter 17
Others On His Doorstep

Field's words had been an inspiration to readers, but his life and death were an inspiration as well. Poets, authors, preachers, bird watchers, and others found their way to the serenity of one or the other of his gravesites.

Some just came to pay their respects. Others penned poetic tributes or biographies. Still others critiqued his work or commented on his noteworthy place in the world of literature.

Most agreed that Eugene Field had written some great poems, particularly his lullabies, and, most especially "Little Boy Blue," his tribute to his lost children. As Slason Thompson, the publisher of Field's extremely popular *Little Book of Western Verse*, said: If that book contained no other poem than "Little Boy Blue," then Eugene Field would still be sure of "immortality." [100]

Today, many critics consider "Little Boy Blue" a classic, and it has even become a collector's item. A little more than twenty years after Eugene Field died, his friend Slason Thompson donated the original hand-written, sketch-illustrated, "Little Boy Blue" manuscript to an auction, to raise money to benefit the allies in World War I. Ironically, that poem about toy soldiers and the death of a son—written by a man who hated war and violence—was actually used to raise money to help fight the war that was expected to end all wars.

"Little Boy Blue" raised $2400 for the war effort—quite a substantial sum, especially in those days—and the poem then took on a new identity.

An Irish tenor, a great singer named John McCormack, bought the original manuscript and recorded the poem as a very poignant song.[101]

Several American composers, including the once-popular Reginald DeKoven and Ethelbert Nevin, also set "Little Boy Blue," The "Dutch Lullaby," and other Field poems to music. Those songs became great favorites of the young and the young-at-heart in the early twentieth century.[102]

Chapter 18
Remembering the Poet of Childhood

During Eugene Field's first funeral in 1895, a call was raised to build a monument to the Children's Poet. One of the first was just a plaque or tablet put in place in 1902 at one of Eugene Field's homes in St. Louis.

That plaque says the house was Eugene's birthplace. But younger brother Rosy told Mark Twain, the guest speaker during the ceremony, that he believed Gene had been born on a different day and on Collins Street (in a house that had since been torn down and replaced by a boiler shop)— not at the house on Broadway Street.

Eugene had used both September 2nd and 3rd

as his birthday, and no one seemed to know if the family had moved from their Collins Street house shortly before or after his birth. Mark Twain said it did not matter and continued the tribute.[103]

In 1919, Denver, Colorado, built the very first park memorial to Eugene Field. That seven-foot tall statue of "Wynken, Blynken, and Nod" still stands there in Washington Park. A copy of that statue, by the same sculptor, Mabel Landrum Torrey, also stands in a park in her other home state of Pennsylvania, in the town of Wellsboro.

In 1922, almost thirty years after Field's death, a statue called "The Rock-a-By Lady from Hush-a-By Street" came to stand in Lincoln Park in Chicago. Money for that project was raised through donations from children and other friends over the years. Soon after that, six or more U.S. cities made plans to build monuments of their own to the Children's Poet.[104]

People did not want to forget Eugene Field or the fact that he had lived in those places, but the times were changing, and so were the neighborhoods. Sadly, three years later, in 1925, the wrecking ball demolished Field's beloved Sabine Farm house in Chicago so that an eight-story apartment house could take its place.

Then in 1927, Field's "cottage" on Colfax Avenue was rescued from demolition by Denver's socialite Titanic-survivor "The Unsinkable Molly Brown," who loved Eugene Field's works. She had the cottage moved to Washington Park where it became a branch of the Denver Public Library and where it now stands near the 1919 statue of "Wynken, Blynken, and Nod."[105]

Around the same time, St. Joseph began to collect and preserve the Field family manuscripts and other papers. Other cities, universities, and libraries would also develop Field Collections.[106]

How ironic it now seems that Eugene Field, the doorstep orphan so often shuttled off to family, friends, or strangers, in life, had become the beloved poet of childhood claimed by so many cities and states, after his death. And now, far more than a century later, he is generally remembered only by those monuments in his honor and by the everlasting words of the poems he wrote.

"Little Boy Blue," in particular, still speaks and sings to the hearts of men, women, and children everywhere. An especially timeless poem of love and longing, it is one of Eugene Field's very best, but it is not his only popular poem.

"Little Boy Blue" and the other two poems contained in this little book, the "Dutch Lullaby" (or "Wynken, Blynken, and Nod") and "The Duel" (or "the Gingham Dog and the Calico Cat"), are now generally considered Field's best-known and best-loved works.[107]

Those poems were written from his heart, from his memories, and from his love for children and parents. No matter when they were written, they speak directly to the hearts of readers of all ages.

As in this poem written for his foster-mother and cousin Mary Field French, they bid readers to:

Take…these little children of his pen

And love them for the author's sake,

just as readers for far more than one hundred years have loved them—as perhaps the greatest and best-known works of Eugene Field, "The poet of Childhood" and "The Children's Poet."[108]

THE END

Selected Field Sites

- Several states have Eugene Field Elementary Schools and Public Libraries
- Colorado, Denver: Poet's Row Apartments, Eugene Field House
- Colorado, Denver: Washington Park, Field Cottage and "Wynken, Blynken, and Nod" statue
- Illinois, Chicago: Albany Park, Eugene Field Fieldhouse and Park http://www.yelp.com/biz/eugene-field-park-chicago http://stage.chicagoparkdistrict.duodesign.com/index.cfm/fuseaction/parks.detail/object_id/abb8ea43-8d7c-4cd6-99bc-0fc6fec64245.cfm
- Illinois, Chicago: Eugene Field Memorial Reliefs http://www.waymarking.com/waymarks/WM8TJ0_Eugene_Field_Memorial_reliefs_Chicago_IL
- Illinois, Chicago: Graceland Cemetery, original gravesite of Eugene Field
- Illinois, Chicago: Kenilworth Cemetery, Eugene Field grave
- Illinois, Chicago: Lincoln Park Zoo, "Dream Lady Statue" or "The Rock-a-By Lady of Hush-a-By Street"
- Illinois, Oak Park: Eugene Field Park
- Massachusetts, Amherst: University of Massachusetts, Orchard Hill Residence Hall, Eugene Field Dormitory
- Missouri, St. Louis: Eugene Field House/Roswell Field House http://www.visitmo.com/eugene-field-house.aspx
- Missouri, St. Louis: Eugene Field House and St. Louis Toy Museum: National register, St. Louis Landmark, includes Dred Scott/Roswell Field resources http://www.eugenefieldhouse.org/ http://www.eugenefieldhouse.org/index.php?option=com_content&view=article&id=56&Itemid=74
- Missouri, St. Louis: Eugene Field Memorial Tablet (or plaque) http://www.twainquotes.com/Steamboats/EugeneField.html
- Missouri, St. Louis: Walk of Fame, Star for Eugene Field http://www.stlouiswalkoffame.org/inductees/eugene-field.html
- Pennsylvania, Wellsboro; on the Green, Statue of "Wynken, Blynken, and Nod" or the "Dutch Lullaby" twin statue to the one in Denver's Washington Park

Reference List

Below, Ida Comstock. *Eugene Field in His Home*. New York: Dutton, 1898. A short biography of Eugene Field, focusing on his home and family, written by his wife's sister Ida Comstock.

Borland, Kathryn Kilby and Helen Ross Speicher. *Eugene Field: Young Poet*. Indianapolis: Bobbs-Merrill, 1964. A long but easy to read children's biography of Eugene Field's growing up years from the much loved Bobbs-Merrill "Childhood of" series.

Brenner, Rica. *Twelve American Poets Before 1900*. New York: Harcourt Brace & Company, 1933. An examination of Field as the perpetual child, his family history, growing up with extended family, academics, his father's sudden death, his journalism career and marriage and ever-increasing family, poems, pranks, souvenir and book collecting, "Little Boy Blue" and other tragic poems, trips to Europe, failing health, death of children, home ownership, and death.

Clemens, Will M., ed, in Eugene Field's *The Stars: A Slumber Story*. New York: New Amsterdam Book Co., 1901. A small three-part book containing "The Stars," a story by Eugene Field, sandwiched between "The Child-Love of Eugene Field: An Appreciation" by his friend Will M. Clemens, and "Eugene Field, a Sketch." The first of those is a biographical/literary criticism and the last is a biographical sketch.

Conrow, Robert. *Field Days: The Life, Times & Reputation of Eugene Field*. New York: Scribner's, 1974. Fairly good timeline, copies of handwritten edited works, and actual photos enhance this biography of Field.

Cunliffe, John W. and Ashley H. Thorndike, Eds. "Eugene Field" in the *Warner Library in Thirty Volumes* [*The World's Best Literature*] Vol. 9. pp. 5687-5692 New York: Knickerbocker Press/Warner Library Company, 1917. Brief biography of Field, by Richard Burton, Professor of English at the University of Minnesota; and three of Field's poems, including the "Dutch Lullaby."

Dennis, Charles H. *Eugene Field's Creative Years*. Garden City, NY: Doubleday, Page, & Co., 1924. A friend and co-worker of twelve years endeavors to discuss Eugene Field's works and adult years.

"Eugene Field." *Encyclopedia Britannica*. 1994.

Field, Eugene. *An Auto-Analysis & the Two Friars*. New York: Caldwell, 1901. The auto-analysis part of this book is a good, simple, quick autobiographical sketch of Field himself and his likes and dislikes.

Field, Eugene. *Little Book of Western Verse.* New York: Scribner's, 1893. Field's best known and most popular collection of works.

Field, Eugene. *The Stars: A Slumber Story.* New York: New Amsterdam Book Co., 1901. A small three-part book containing "The Stars," a story by Eugene Field, sandwiched between "The Child-Love of Eugene Field: An Appreciation" by his friend Will M. Clemens, and "Eugene Field, a Sketch." The first of those is a biographical/literary criticism and the last is a biographical sketch.

Field, Eugene. *With Trumpet and Drum.* New York: Scribner's 1895. Short collection of Field's poems.

Fischer, Henry William and Merle De Vore Johnson. *Abroad with Mark Twain and Eugene Field.* West Richard, 1922. Reprinted from the public domain by Bibliolife (n.p., n. d.). Many vignettes of Twain and a few of Field in Europe as collected by Fischer, a widely traveled and well known newspaperman, who had spent extensive time wih Twain and Field in various cities over three decades as told to Johnson.

Greene, Carol. *Eugene Field: The Children's Poet.* Chicago: Children's Press, 1994. Short, easy-to-read children's level biography of Field with many good photos.

Hart, James D., Ed. "Eugene Field," in *Oxford Companion to American Literature.* 5th ed. New York: Oxford University Press, 1983. A companion book and guide to American literature by a highly trusted source, contains a small section on Field.

Lindley, Lester G. "Lives in Parallel: Dred Scot and One of His Attorneys," A Review of Kenneth C. Kaufman's *Dred Scott's Advocate: A Biography of Roswell M. Field.* H-Law, H-Net Reviews. October, 1997. online at http://www.h-net.org/reviews/showrev.php?id=1385

Meigs, Cornelia, Anne Thaxter Eaton, Elizabeth Nesbitt, and Ruth Hill Viguers. *A Critical History of Children's Literature, Earliest Times to the Present, Prepared in Four Parts under the Editorship of Cornelia Meigs.* New York: MacMillan, 1953. An analysis of Eugene Field's works and his place and contributions to the world of children's literature in America by four experts in that area.

Nolan, Jeannette Covert. *The Gay Poet: The Story of Eugene Field.* New York: Julian Messner, 1940. Although unfortunately named and also fictionalized, this biography of Field is excellent and offers a very human picture of the boy and the man.

Stedman, Edmund Clarence. "Eugene Field," in *Genius and Other Essays*. New York: Moffat, Yard, & Co., 1911. Reprinted Washington, NY: Kennikat Press, 1966.

    Essay about Eugene Field contained within a collection of essays about other men, all written by Stedman who was a writer and a very good friend of Field's. Stedman admired Field and many of his works. They shared good times, jokes and pranks, and sometimes had a friendly rivalry and a bit of a witty war with each other. Stedman mourned his friend greatly, and in this article he did so in much the same way as Hamlet mourned his old mentor/jester Yorick.

Thompson, Slason. *Life of Eugene Field.* New York: D. Appleton, 1927. In-depth biography of Field by his good friend and co-worker Slatson Thompson.

Thompson, Slason. *Eugene Field: A Study in Heredity and Contradictions*. 2 vols. New York: Scribner's, 1901. Two volume set of in-depth information about Eugene Fields, as written by one of his best friends and co-workers.

End Notes

[1] Thompson, *Eugene Field* V2 p 314; Thompson, *Life of Eugene Field*, pp 372-3.
[2] Conrow, p 6; Meigs, p 411.
[3] Below, p 1; Borland, p 193; Conrow, p 2,5, 35; Cunliffe, p 5687; Dennis, pp. 10-11; Field, *Auto-Analysis*, p 47; Nolan, pp 40-1; Thompson, *Eugene Field* V1 pp 50-3; Thompson, *Life of Eugene Field*, pp 15, 257.
[4] Thompson, *Life of Eugene Field*, pp 14-5.
[5] Below, p 16; Greene, p 5.
[6] Greene, p. 6; Borland, p 16.
[7] Below, pp 16, 77.
[8] Dennis, pp. 13-15; Nolan, pp 72-77; Thompson, *Eugene Field* V1, pp 37-44; Lindley.
[9] Borland, p 16; Greene, p 7; Thompson, *Eugene Field* V1, pp 50-1.
[10] Borland, p 19; Thompson, *Eugene Field* V1, pp 52-4; Thompson, *Life of Eugene Field*, pp 16-7, 258.
[11] Thompson, *Eugene Field* V1, pp 8-9, 54.
[12] Thompson, *Life of Eugene Field*, p. 17.
[13] Nolan, pp 37.
[14] Below, pp 22-3; Thompson, *Life of Eugene Field*, pp 17-18.
[15] Below, pp 21-2.
[16] Borland. pp 29-35; Nolan, p 36-7.
[17] Greene, p 8; Stedman, pp 185-6.
[18] Borland, pp 36-39; Greene, pp 9, 11; Nolan, pp 33-6, 41; Thompson, *Life of Eugene Field*, pp 20-1.
[19] Greene, p 12; Nolan, p. 17.
[20] Thompson, *Eugene Field* V2 pp 299-301.
[21] Field, *Auto-Analysis*, p 59; Nolan, p 24.
[22] Greene, p 13; Nolan, p 28; Thompson, *Eugene Field* V1, p 69.
[23] Nolan, p 29.
[24] Nolan, pp 29-31.
[25] Nolan, p 30.
[26] Below, p 6; Nolan, p 43-6.
[27] Thompson, *Life of Eugene Field*, pp 7-8.
[28] Nolan, p 47.
[29] Borland, p 96; Greene, p 11.
[30] Borland, pp 63-4, 67-8.

[31] Borland, pp 99, 104-5; Clemens, *The Stars*, p 68-9; Nolan, pp 50-1.
[32] Borland, pp 77, 92; Nolan, pp 53-5.
[33] Thompson, *Eugene Field* V1, pp 1-12; *Life of Eugene Field*, pp 5-7.
[34] Below, pp 11-16; Thompson, *Eugene Field* V1, pp 9-12; Thompson, *Life of Eugene Field*, p 1.
[35] Nolan, pp 72-77; Thompson, *Eugene Field* V1, pp 13-35; Thompson, *Life of Eugene Field*, pp 3, 10-2.
[36] Dennis, pp. 13-15.
[37] Lindley.
[38] Field, *Auto Analysis*, p 59; Nolan, pp 72-7; Thompson, *Eugene Field* V2, pp 243-4.
[39] Thompson, *Eugene Field* V1, pp 74-8.
[40] Borland, pp 151-156; Nolan, pp 81, 92-6; Thompson, *Life of Eugene Field*, p 29.
[41] Borland, pp 151-156; Nolan, pp 81, 92-6; Thompson, *Life of Eugene Field*, p 29.
[42] Greene, p 17.
[43] Thompson, *Life of Eugene Field*, p 258.
[44] Nolan, p 98.
[45] Thompson, *Life of Eugene Field*, p 30.
[46] Below, p 25; Clemens, *The Stars*, p 54-5.
[47] Lindley; Thompson, *Life of Eugene Field*, p 13.
[48] Nolan, pp 111-2.
[49] Nolan, p 115.
[50] Thompson, *Eugene Field* V1, pp 91-2; Thompson, *Life of Eugene Field*, p 30.
[51] Below, pp 35-37.
[52] Thompson, *Eugene Field*, pp 94-96.
[53] Thompson, *Life of Eugene Field*, p 36.
[54] Below, pp 37-8; Thompson, *Life of Eugene Field*, p 42.
[55] Clemens, The Stars, pp 58-9; Thompson, *Eugene Field* V1, pp 99-100
[56] Below, p 39; Borland, p 178.
[57] Thompson, *Life of Eugene Field*, p 44.
[58] Conrow, p. 68; Thompson, *Eugene Field* V1, pp 56, 109-11.
[59] Fischer, pp 226, 230; Conrow, pp 68-9; Nolan, p 188; Thompson, *Eugene Field* V2, p 6.
[60] Nolan, pp. 170, 172-3.
[61] Below, p 50.

[62] Nolan, p 191.
[63] Thompson, *Life of Eugene Field*, p 348.
[64] Thompson, *Eugene Field* V1, p129.
[65] Nolan, p 191.
[66] Conrow, p. 68; Thompson, *Eugene Field* V1, p. 122.
[67] Conrow, pp. 191-2; Nolan, pp 225-6; Thompson, *Eugene Field*, V2, pp 110-115.
[68] Thompson, *Eugene Field* V2, pp 110, 112.
[69] Dennis, pp 39, 200.
[70] Fischer, p 246.
[71] Conrow, p 6; Thompson, *Eugene Field* V2, pp 121-2.
[72] Nolan, pp 228-9.
[73] Thompson, *Life of Eugene Field*, pp 374-5.
[74] Thompson, *Eugene Field* V1, p 136; V2, pp 137, 234; Thompson, *Life of Eugene Field*, p 61
[75] Nolan, pp 231-3; Thompson, *Eugene Field* V2, pp 138-168.
[76] Nolan, pp 231-3; Thompson, *Eugene Field* V2, pp 138-168.
[77] Nolan, pp 231-3; Thompson, *Eugene Field* V2, pp 138-168.
[78] Thompson, *Eugene Field* V2, pp 160-1.
[79] Field, *Auto-Analysis*, p 51; Cunliffe, p 5687.
[80] Greene, pp 33, 35.
[81] Nolan, pp 240-244.
[82] Below, p 30; Conrow, p 14; Greene, p 27; Nolan, pp 240-3, 245.
[83] Cunliffe, p 5687.
[84] Nolan, p 229.
[85] Conrow, p 187.
[86] Clemens, *The Stars*, pp 62-3.
[87] Below, pp 30-1; Nolan, p 37; Thompson, *Life of Eugene Field*, pp 341, 346-351.
[88] Nolan, pp 228, 252; Thompson, *Eugene Field* V2, pp 1, 311.
[89] Dennis, p 328; Thompson, *Life of Eugene Field*, p 365.
[90] Conrow, pp 11-2; Dennis, p 328; Clemens, *The Stars*, p 70.
[91] Thompson, *Eugene Field* V2, pp 311-2.
[92] Conrow, p 17; Nolan, p 229.
[93] Conrow, p 22; Greene, p 45; Thompson, *Eugene Field* V2, pp 315-6.
[94] Thompson, *Life of Eugene Field*, pp 348-9.
[95] Thompson, *Life of Eugene Field*, pp 370-1.
[96] Conrow, pp 34-7.
[97] Conrow, pp 34-7; Greene, p 44.

[98] Thompson, *Life of Eugene Field*, p 371.
[99] Conrow, pp 228-9.
[100] Thompson, *Life of Eugene Field*, pp 374-5.
[101] Thompson, *Life of Eugene Field*, p 375.
[102] Hart, p 247.
[103] Conrow, pp 49, 50, 57; Thompson, *Eugene Field* V1, pp 50-1.
[104] Conrow, pp 9-10, 24, 33-4, 37, 45.
[105] Conrow, pp 47, 52, 53, 69.
[106] Conrow, pp 231-2.
[107] Hart, p 247.
[108] Field, "To Mary Field French," *Little Book of Western Verse*, dedication.

Glossary

Abolitionist: person in the Civil War who worked to free the slaves
affluent: wealthy, rich, high class
calico: cotton cloth often decorated with polka-dots or little squares
curiosity shop: old-fashioned store containing used odds and ends
doorstep orphan: orphan or abandoned child left for others to raise
dreaded: hated to see
esteemed: important
faction-ridden: torn apart by conflicting groups
figuratively: metaphorically speaking; using figures of speech
footstove: old-fashioned portable stove used to keep feet warm
frolic: to run and jump and play
gingham: striped or patterned cotton cloth
Jr.; Junior; younger person with the same name as an older person
literally: in reality or truthfully
lullaby: song or poem used to help a child relax and sleep
lyrics: words of a song or poem
manuscript: typed/written part of a book before it is published
melancholy: very sad or depressed; remembering a better time
menagerie: strange group of different kinds of animals
mischievous: ornery
nostalgia: a yearning for a past time or place
outbuildings: barns, sheds, or other unattached buildings
parody: a humorous rework of a poem or song
Peter Pan: hero of lost children; a boy who refuses to grow up
pewter: tin-like metal used for figurines, such as toy soldiers, etc.
Puritan: very strict early American religion
recluse (reclusive): hermit (or hermit-like)
row: a fight
satire or satirical: type of writing that makes fun of something
scholar: a serious and intelligent student
shoe-button: button once commonly used to fasten a shoe
souvenir: item bought to remember a trip, special time, or event
spinster: unmarried woman; old maid
Sr.: Senior; older person with the same name as a younger person
staunch: loyal
stipulations: requirements
trundle-bed: a pull-out bed for children, kept under an adult's bed
Unionist: someone who works to maintain the federal government
waif: an orphan or stray; a poor little girl

Index

Amherst, Massachusetts, 6.
America, 5.
"April Vespers," 39.
Armenia, 55.
Belgium, 49.
Broadway Street, 75.
Brown, "The Unsinkable" Molly, 77.
Buena Park, 63.
Chicago, Illinois, 28, 41, 50, 52, 63, 66, 68, 70, 76, 77.
Chicago Tribune, 66.
"Christmas Treasures," 38, 42.
Civil War, 5, 10, 21, 22, 23, 24.
Collins Street, 75, 76.
Colfax Avenue, 77.
Colorado, 76.
Comstock, Edgar, 30, 31, 32-33, 37.
Comstock, Ida (Ida Comstock Below), 33.
Comstock, Julia (see Field, Julia Comstock)
Comstock family, 30, 31, 33.
Cornwall, 55.
DeKoven, Reginald, 74.
Denver, Colorado, 28, 52, 76, 77.
Dickinson, Emily, 7, 8.
Dickinson, Lavinia, 7.
Dooley, 18.
Doyle, Sir Arthur Conan, 49.
Dred Scott Case, 5, 22-23.
"The Duel" ("Gingham Dog and the Calico Cat"), 2, 13, 14-16, 48, 50, 78.
"Dutch Lullaby" ("Wynken, Blynken, and Nod"), 2, 48, 55, 56-59, 60, 66, 74, 78.
England, 49, 55.
Ethan, Mrs., 11-12, 13, 54.
Europe, 11, 30, 31, 33, 34, 39, 49.

Field, Esther Kellogg (Grandmother), 17, 18, 19, 20, 21, 24, 25-29, 30, 52, 54, 62, 63, 75.
Field, Eugene, 1, 2-15, 17-35, 37-42, 44, 48-50, 52, 54-55, 60-70, 72-73, 75-79.
Field, Eugene, Jr. ("Pinny"), 40, 63.
Field, Frances Reed (Mother), 4, 5, 21, 28.
Field, Frederick ("Daisy"), 40, 63, 64.
Field, Julia Comstock (Wife), 31-35, 37, 49, 63, 70.
Field, Mary French ("Trotty"), 39, 63.
Field, Melvin Gray (Son), 30, 39.
Field, Roswell Francis ("Posy"), 52, 63.
Field, Roswell Martin (Eugene's first son), 38.
Field, Roswell Martin, Jr. (Eugene's brother Rosy), 3-4, 7, 11-12, 13, 17, 19, 21, 24, 25-29, 30, 52, 54, 63, 75.
Field, Roswell Martin, Sr. (Eugene's father), 4, 5, 6, 10, 17, 18, 20, 21, 22, 23, 24, 28, 29, 30, 32, 38, 43, 52, 65.
Field, Ruth Gray ("Sister Girl"), 52, 63.
France, 34, 49.
French, Mary Field ("Cousin Mary"), 6, 7, 8, 11-12, 13, 18, 21, 25, 30, 33, 38-39, 48, 79.
Galesburg, Illinois, 29.
Germany, 49, 50.
Gilbert, Sir William S., 39, 40.
Gilbert and Sullivan, 39, 40.
"Gingham Dog and the Calico Cat" ("The Duel"), 2, 13, 14-16, 78.
Graceland Cemetery, 68.
Gray, Melvin, 30, 35, 39.
H.M.S. Pinafore, 40.
Hawthorne, Julian, 41.
Hawthorne, Nathaniel, 41.
Holland, 49.
Illinois, 29, 63.
Ireland, 34.
Italy, 34.

Japan, 55.
Jones, Mary Field ("Aunt Mary"), 6, 8, 9, 13, 18, 25, 30, 33, 62.
Kansas City, 28, 52.
Kenilworth Cemetery, 70, 71.
Knox College, 27, 29, 30.
Lincoln, President Abraham, 23, 24.
Lincoln Park, 69, 76.
Little Book of Profitable Tales, 48.
Little Book of Western Verse, 48, 49, 73.
"Little Boy Blue," 2, 38, 43, 44, 45-47, 48, 49, 50, 51, 66, 70, 72, 73, 74, 78.
McCormack, John, 74.
Massachusetts, 6, 24.
Missouri, 3, 5, 21, 23, 27, 29, 30, 33.
Monson, Massachusetts, 24, 37, 28.
Nevin, Ethelbert, 74.
New England, 17, 20.
New York, 33, 35.
Newfane, Vermont, 18.
Norway, 55.
"Oh My! Ain't He a Daisy," 40.
Orkney, 55.
Pennsylvania, 76.
Peter Pan, 35.
Phelps, Mary Almira, 21.
Puritan, 17, 20.
"Rock-a-By Lady from Hush-a-By Street," 76.
Sabine Farm, 63, 77.
St. Joseph, Missouri, 28, 30, 32, 33, 52, 77.
St. Louis, Missouri, 3, 4, 28, 34, 52, 75.
Scot, Dred, 5, 22-23.
Scotland, 49, 55.
"Sharps and Flats," 66.
Sicily, 55.

Spencer, Deacon, 23.
Sullivan, Sir Arthur, 39-40.
Thompson, Slason, 35, 43, 48, 50, 65, 68, 69, 72, 73.
Titanic, 77.
Torrey, Mabel Landrum, 76.
Tufts, Reverend James, 24, 28.
Twain, Mark, 75-76.
University of Missouri, 27, 29, 30.
Vermont, 18, 21.
Washington Park, 76.
Wellsboro, Pennsylvania, 76, 77.
Wilde, Oscar, 49.
Williams College, 26, 27, 28.
With Trumpet and Drum, 50.
"Wynken, Blynken, and Nod" ("Dutch Lullaby"), 2, 38, 55, 56-59, 66, 76, 77, 78.
"Wynken, Blynken, and Nod" (statue), 76, 77.

About the Author

Dr. Jean A. Lukesh
(M.A.Ed., History; M.A.Ed. English;
Ed.D., Curriculum & Instruction;
Graduate, Denver University Publishing Institute)

Jean Lukesh worked for thirty years as a public school Librarian, Media Specialist, Integration Specialist, Technology Representative, and classroom Teacher. She is probably best known for her popular Reluctant Reader booktalks and American History books. Now retired from everyday teaching, she writes, edits, and publishes books for children and adults, gives history and writing presentations and workshops, and mentors other authors.

Her *Nebraska Adventure*, a 4th grade Nebraska Studies textbook (©2004, 2005), is very popular with children, teachers, and other adults of all ages. Awards for that book include the 2005 national Texty Award for Excellence in El-Hi Humanities/Social Sciences, the 2006 Nebraska Center for the Book Award, and the 2006 Moonshell Arts and Humanities Council's Children's Nonfiction Award.

Working with fellow Nebraskan Ben Kuroki, she then wrote *Lucky Ears: The True Story of Ben Kuroki, World War II Hero* (©2010). That is the first book in her Noteworthy Americans series of Quick Reader biographies for kids 10 to 110. In 2011, *Lucky Ears* received two national/international Bronze Medals in Book Award competition for Multicultural Nonfiction for Children/Teens/Young Adults. Two other books in that series were published in late 2011/early 2012. They are *Sky Rider: The Story of Evelyn Sharp, World War II WASP* and *Wolves in Blue: Stories of the North Brothers and Their Pawnee Scouts*

Dr. Lukesh has received many other honors and awards including the Nebraska Library Association's 2010 Mari Sandoz Award.

www.ingramcontent.com/pod-product-compliance
Lightning Source LLC
Chambersburg PA
CBHW060207050426
42446CB00013B/3016